C000295349

Till we Meet Again

ℛℛ

RAVETTE PUBLISHING

First published in 2014 by
Ravette Publishing Limited
PO Box 876, Horsham
West Sussex RH12 9GH

ISBN: 978-1-84161-383-3

WE SHALL WANT YOU AND MISS YOU

THERE they go, our gallant soldiers, marching
    forth to win or die,
Dad's amongst them, sonny darling—wave to him
    as he goes by,
For he'll love to see us watching—love to catch a
    parting view,
Twill be sweet for him to think of, when he's far
    from me and you.

·MADELEINE ST. CLAIR·

*D*EAR DADDY, *every night I'm going to pray*
That God will keep you safe while you're away.

Keep Him ever in Thy Care

GOD bless my Dad this eventide, and ever more,
    I pray,
And keep him safe from every harm, while he is
    far away ;
For tho' we cannot reach him, he's very close
    to Thee,
And Thou can'st see him where he is, just as
    Thou seest me ;
O, link us up—Dad, Mum, and me,—with chains
    of fondest love,
Then Dad won't feel alone <u>one bit</u>, if we are
    linked above.

BAMFORTH (Copyright)   MADELEINE ST CLAIR.

Please, Mamma, tell me where my Daddy's gone.

A Cherished Thought of Dad

I am thinking of Daddy, and wishing
    him here,
On this bright Sabbath morning, with us,
    Mammy dear ;
But I feel he is close, though his dear face
    we miss,
So just kiss me once more with a " Daddy's
    own kiss."

Love From Home

LADDIE, we're missing you,
Laddie, we think of you,
Laddie, we pray for you,
Laddie, we're proud of you!

Fondest love to all at home

Tho' we're parted, dearest parents, sisters, brothers,
      loved ones true,
There will come a day of blessing,
      re-uniting me to you,
This is not a time for sorrow – joy with duty
      goes in hand.
Soon will come a bright to-morrow,
      shedding sunshine o'er the land.

BAMFORTH (Copyright)   MADELEINE ST. CLAIR.

Fond Remembrance

Think not because of absence, lad,
  You're e'er forgotten here :
God knows the hearts that beat as one,
  And gently draws them near.

~ Love to Daddy. ~

I AM writing to my Daddy, and I've got just
    lots to say,
Tho' I don't know how to put it down in quite
    the proper way ;
But I love him, and I miss him, and I'm
    proud he's gone to fight,
And I mean to grow up just like him—that's
    what I <u>want</u> to write.—

Thoughts Sincere
and Wishes True

GOD knoweth how I miss you, dear,
  Yet Hope oft bids my thoughts to stray,
To all the happiness in store,
  When you've come back, one happy day.

I WANT TO KISS MY SOLDIER DADDY

ME can't be <u>always</u> laughing, all the night and
all the day,
I's tinking of my Daddy, and he <u>is so</u> far away;
Big tears <u>will</u> come altho' I twy to be so good, and smile,
But I <u>must</u> tink of Dad dis way, just evwy lickle while.

·MADELEINE ST. CLAIR.

A LINE TO FATHER.

HERE'S A LINE TO MY DEAR DAD, JUST TO SAY I'M BLOOMING,

BUSINESS—WELL; IT ISN'T BAD, FACT I'D CALL IT BOOMING.

MAKES YOU WELL, AND KEEPS YOU FIT, STOPS YOU GETTING DREAMY.

TELL YOU, DAD, THE LIFE IS **IT**—WAIT UNTIL YOU SEE ME.—*Madeleine St. Clair.*

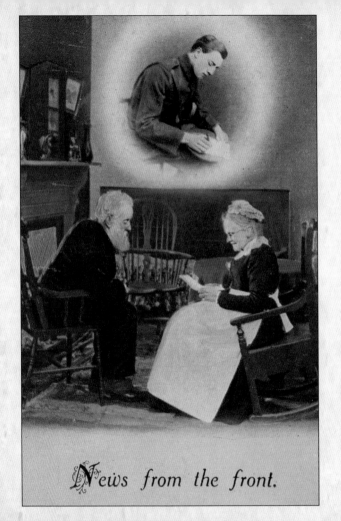

News from the front.

Tenderest thoughts of Thee

Far away in the land I love, oft in thought
                    I fondly rove,
Gaze into eyes that sparkle bright, with a
                    welcoming love-light,
Kiss the fond lips that bade adieu—
          laughing now with joy anew
Clasp to my heart the form so dear,
          ne'er to part for many a year.

MADELEINE. ST. CLAIR.

To Greet the Lad I'm Proud of

This is the word I send you—
　　And it is what I fain
Would say if I could but meet you,
　　And clasp your hand again,—
Good luck be your companion,
　　Good health be yours to stay,
And all that makes for happiness
　　Attend you, day by day.

BAMFORTH (Copyright)　　　　　　　　MADELEINE ST CLAIR

*There is ever and ever so much to say
When I write to my soldier far away;
Perhaps I shall tell it all some day!*

Greetings to my loved ones at home.

Here's a greeting to my loved ones,
      just to say all's well with me,
And to tell them I am thinking
      of the home I'd love to see.
Cares there are—yet sweet the knowledge
      that one holds a place apart,
Very warm and very tender, in each
      faithful loving heart.

MADELEINE St. CLAIR.

Happy Thoughts

Each of us misses the One that's away,
  Each of us longs so for that happy day,
When, partings all over and hearts made glad,
We'll all be together,—dog, lass and lad.

MADELEINE ST. CLAIR.

NEWS FROM HOME, SWEET HOME.

I · Never · Forget · you · Lad ·

As I look at your portrait, laddie,
    It always would seem to say—
"Cheer up, dear Mother, I'm doing my bit,
    And we'll meet again, someday;"
Then my old heart throbs with love and pride,
    For the son who's far away.

MADELEINE ST CLAIR.

Loving Thoughts of Dad.

We miss you, Daddy, ever so,
    But you are out to fight the foe;
Oh, we would be brave soldiers. too,
And grow up, Daddy, just like you.

—MADE! EINE ST. CLAIR.

Love from
Daddy's Little Girl

Lickle baby's always tinking she can hear her
    Dadda speak,
Always he's around the corners—always playing hide
    and seek ;
Mamma says she seems to see him—sees him a'most
    all the day,
Guess if babs could only catch him, he should never
    get away.

MADELEINE ST. CLAIR.

Writing a Letter to Daddy

I am so lonely, for you are away,
So I shan't have fine romps and
your kisses to-day;
But I hope you are happy
(I promise to be),
And that soon you'll come back to dear
Mother and me.

To my dear ones at home

Far away to the homeland dear
My fancy strays in the hour of rest,
Again I see in vision clear
The forms of those whom I love best.

BAMFORTH. (Copyright)   MADELEINE ST CLAIR.

WRITING A LETTER TO DADDY.

To Greet the Dad We're Proud Of

SOMETIMES we two get dreaming, toward the
       close of day,
And in the realms of seeming, we're with you—far
       away,
Then joy, untinged by sadness, soothes every breath
       of pain,
And kissing in our gladness, we wake to hope again.

—MADELEINE ST. CLAIR.

I Loves my Dad

DAT'S my Daddy's picture, an' I'm feeling awful
   proud,
'Cos my Dad's a soldier, where the guns are firing
   loud ;
Guess he's awful brave an' fine, an' fights the
   whole long day,
So's to keep us safe an' sound, an' drive all harm
   away.

MADELEINE ST CLAIR.

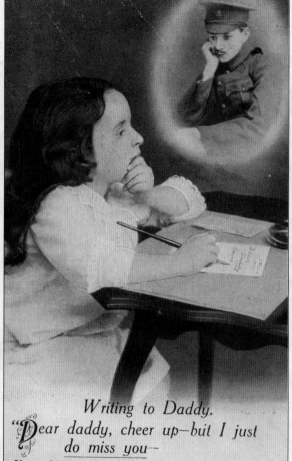

Writing to Daddy.

"*Dear daddy, cheer up—but I just
do miss you—*
I'm always longing to hug and kiss you."

She longs for her daddy to come once more,
When the fight is won and the strife
is o'er.

To Our Daddy Brave.

O God, please bless our Daddy brave,
  Who's more than we can tell
To Mam and us,—and keep him safe
  From every shot and shell;
And when he's won the great big war,
  Please send him back, quite well.

Memories

DADDY'S photo, why don't you talk to me and
play,
Just like my own Daddy did, 'fore he went away?
Still, I guess as you're like Dad, you've got _lots_
to do,
Maybe _that's_ why you don't talk, tho' _I_ talks to _you_

MADELEINE ST. CLAIR.

Sweet Thoughts

Tho' far from thee in body,
  My spirit often seems
With thine, in sweet communion,
  Both waking, and in dreams.

MADELEINE ST. CLAIR.

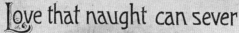

Love that naught can sever

On the wings of swift fancy my thoughts fly away
To a dear little home in the west,
Where my bairnies and Dear one are waiting the day
Which will bring them the one they love best.

BAMFORTH. (Copyright)   MADELLINE St CLAIR.

God Bless Daddy

O GOD, please bless my Daddy dear, wherever he
        may be,
And send him back quite safe and sound to my dear
        Mum and me;
For oh, we love him very much—he is so good and kind,
And Mummy says where love is strong there's links in
        Heaven that bind;
O, make them firm and tight, and shield my Dad from
        shot and shell,
And tell him how I miss him,—'cause I can't write
        very well.

MADELEINE ST. CLAIR.

Cheer up, mother, I'll look after you

TO AN OLD CHUM

Just a hasty line or two,
  Our friendship warm resuming,
I send, old chum, to-day to you,
  And hope it finds you blooming.
I'm sure that you'll be glad to hear
  I'm getting on real well;
I'm learning how to bayonet,
  And handling shot and shell.

Constance A. Dubois.

Till we Meet Again

I look at your portrait, dear laddie,
  And to it I often say—
"You're playing a hero's part, I know,
  In a country far away;"
And soothe all fears with trust and faith,
  For we'll meet somehow, someday.

MADELEINE ST CLAIR.

Other Bamforth titles available …

	ISBN	Price
World War One Series:		
Memories (book of song cards)	978-1-84161-384-0	£5.99
Saucy Seaside Humour:		
Love Will Find A Way	978-1-84161-367-3	£5.99
Down with Drink	978-1-84161-368-0	£5.99
That's the Way To Do It!	978-1-84161-372-7	£5.99
Not a Care in the World	978-1-84161-373-4	£5.99

HOW TO ORDER:

Please send a cheque/postal order in £ sterling, made payable to
'Ravette Publishing' for the cover price of the book/s and allow the
following for post & packing …

UK & BFPO	70p for the first book & 40p per book thereafter
Europe & Eire	£1.30 for the first book & 70p per book thereafter
Rest of the world	£2.20 for the first book & £1.10 per book thereafter

RAVETTE PUBLISHING LTD
PO Box 876, Horsham, West Sussex   RH12 9GH
Tel: 01403 711443   Fax: 01403 711554
www.ravettepublishing.tel   Email: info@ravettepub.co.uk

Prices and availability are subject to change without prior notice